N   N   S

     I   I   T

          B   B   E

N   I   B   L   E   T   S

          B   E   E

     I   T   T

N   S   S

ISBN: 0-7596-6400-5 (ebook)
ISBN: 0-7596-6401-3 (Paperback)

This book is printed on acid free paper.

1stBooks - rev. 9/27/02

NIBLETS

FOR LOIS
True and Magnetic North

INTRODUCTION

The title of this modest volume announces the fact that its contents are small, corny, and essentially tasteless (indeed, "Nit Wit" was a title reluctantly discarded by the author). A "gentle" reader may find the flavor of these niblets a trifle bitter: cynical, sexist and misanthropic. Political correctness is everywhere absent. Worse, these acrid trifles are all word-plays of the kind that confuse some and irritate many. Their prime virtue is that they are short; not even one-liners: half-liners. If you don't like one or one hundred of them, at least you will not have wasted much time. Can you say that of any other book? Or of the rest of your life, for that matter?

A suggestion: do not savor too many of these niblets at one time. The toothsome becomes tiresome. Ambrose Bierce, author of *The Devil's Dictionary*, once reviewed another's work with the single phrase, "The covers of this book are too far apart." If you treat each of the pages that follow as a single volume you may spare your tastebuds for another day. Plus, you will have bought 103 books for the price of one!

The object of the corn-cob in your hand is to elicit a frequent smile, an occasional laugh and a recurrent wince. These pages are intended to make you neither wise, nor thin, nor in any way a better person. If you seek only books that are good for you, go read a banana.

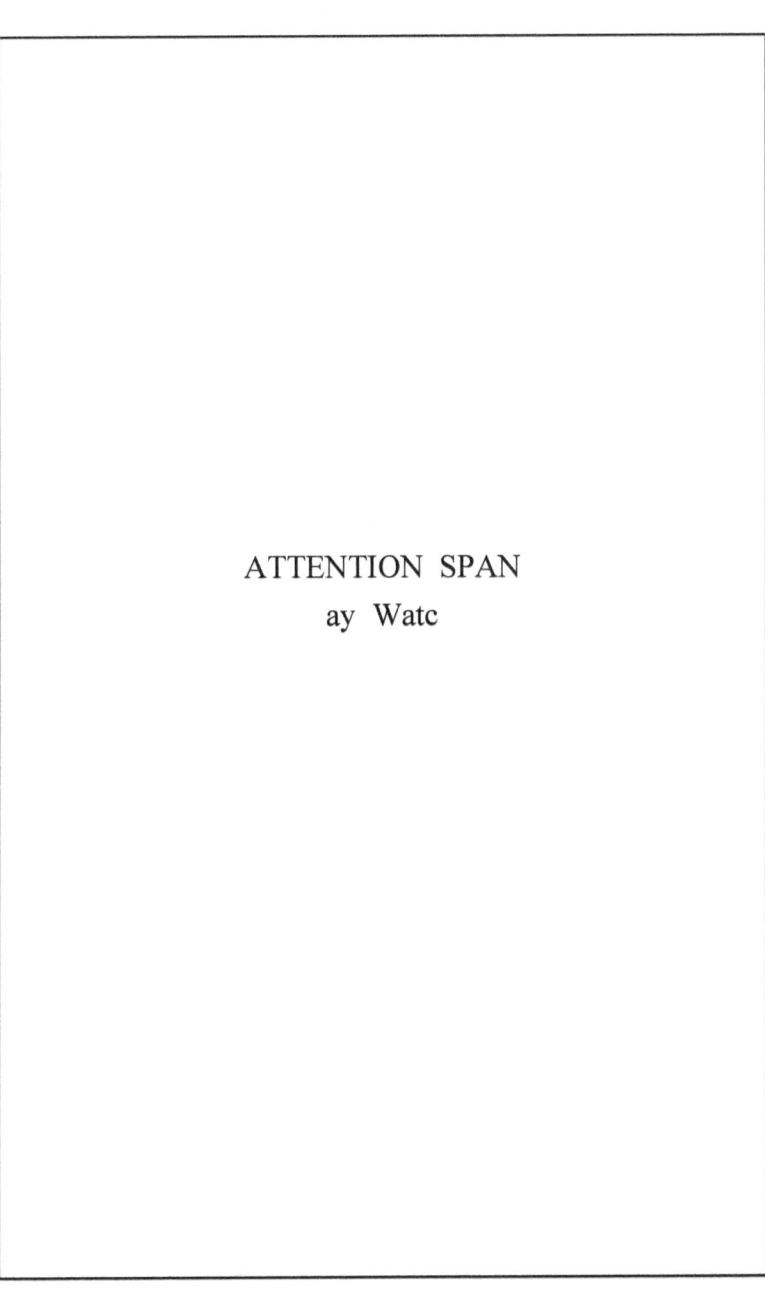

ATTENTION SPAN
ay Watc

THE BOY SCOUTS
A neo - knotsy organization

*

ROMANCE IN THE NURSING HOME
Carbon dating

*

FALLEN KNIGHT
Sir had a gal

*

FLATTERY
Aphrodisiyak

BISEXUALITY
Now you she it, now you don't

*

IF I WERE A CARPENTER,
AND YOU WERE A LADY
Chipboard romance

*

SHOTGUN WEDDING
To rifle with one's affections

*

THE YES MAN SNAPS
Can't get it "yup" any more

YOU'VE GOT A SWAY ABOUT YOU
Bawdy language

*

SKIN TIGHT
Breeches of promise

*

34 - 22 - **36**
20 - 20 hindsight

*

SEDUCTION
Love and mirage

PRE - NUPTIAL JITTERS
Down to the "why her?"

*

THE CEREMONY
Much I do's about nothing

*

THE HONEYMOON IS OVER
The plight at the end of the tunnel

*

POST - NUPTIAL
Rice - a - Ruini

THE GODDESS OF MARITAL LOVE
Aphroduty

*

THE SAD CASE OF THE DYSLEXIC LOVER
96

*

MASTERS AND JOHNSON
We the peep - hole, in order to form
a more perfect union

*

THE FLING
Tried untrue

DON JUAN'S GOODNIGHT
Buenas notches

*

BRIEF UPDATE
From her to attornety

*

DIVORCE
To halve and have not

*

RETURN ENGAGEMENT
Demons are forever

CAPON

Cock - a - toodle - oo

*

FAILED POET

Un - requoted love

*

OZYMANDIAS

Statue of limitations

*

PC MOBY

Dead Right Whale

ROCKER 'ROUND THE CLOCK
Rock and stroll is here to stay, I dig it to the end.

*

WATCHIN' DE TIME GO AWAY
Sittin' on de dock of decay

*

BEAUTICIAN'S EPITAPH
The rest is salons...

*

REINCARNATION
Haven't I been herbivore?

VIRTUE
One night - stand

*

VIRTUE'S REWARD
Past perfect, tense

*

NICE GIRLS FINISH LAST
Winsome, lose some

*

HABITUAL VICTIM
Marching to the drum of a different beater

VOYEURISM
Windows of opportunity

*

VOYEURISM
To peek one's curiosity

*

VOYEURISM
Eye Sigh

*

LE VOYEUR
Le bureau de ma tante est sur la plume de mon oncle

VOYEUR'S AIM
To catch underwears

*

STRIP TEASE
Venetian blonde

*

THE VOYEUR IN LOVE
She's one in a mullion

*

APOLOGIA PRO VOYEUR
At least he does windows

FRESHMAN COMP

It was a stark and dormy night...

*

DOLL HELL

Barbie - queue

*

TIDEOLOGY

Godliness is next to Cleanliness

*

MADISON AVENUE

It's a jingle out there

THE WRITING ON THE WALL
Scrypt

*

AFFAIRS OF THE HEART
Fluttery will get you nowhere

*

THANATOPHILIA
Hot to rot

*

THE FOUNTAIN OF TRUTH
Whither, thou goest

THE POMPOUS LOVER
Opines away

*

THE HESITANT WOOER
ON THE RIVER CAM
When in punt, doubt

*

REGRET
Wince upon a time

*

CYNIC OVERLOOK
Perspeakacidly

IN THE CLOSET
A suit of armoire

*

UNDERCOVER IN TEHERAN
Ch'adore ça

*

OUTED
The hid parade

*

SEE - THROUGH
Man nippulation

DRACULA
Neckromancer

*

THE JOLLY VAMPIRE
An instinct for the jocular

*

NECROPHILIAC'S NIGHTMARE
To take a breather

*

ELMOWEEN THE 13TH
Déjà Boo!

TRY AND TRY AGAIN
Practet makes perfice

*

FLAT LINE
The tunnel at the end of the light

*

OPTIMISM
Myhopeia

*

THE REPENTANT OPTIMIST
The glass is half - full of shit

DEATH AND THE MAIDEN
Va - va - Boom!!

*

MARILYN
Ex object

*

JAYNE
00 - 39 - 26 - 38

*

00 - 00 - 00
A perfect zen

EGO
I there! Pleased to me you!

*

FETISHIST1
1. Foot-noter

*

ANALYSAND
Deep - Freud couch potato

*

PSYCHIATRIST'S CREDO
I shrink therefore I sham

ADULT GAMES
Spin the Battle and *Pist Office*

*

THE BATTLE OF THE SEXES
Plaisir d'armour

*

LET THEM EAT CAKE
Treacle - down economics

*

FILTHY RICH
The effluent society

THE CYNIC'S WORKOUT
Pumping irony

*

NEGATIVE ATTITUDE
Nope problem

*

CARPE DIEM
Tempus, fug it

*

WHIRL WEARY
The whole nonchilada

SISYPHUS
Rock and roll is here to stay

＊

WHICH CAME FIRST,
THE CHICKEN OR THE EGG?
A la recherche du temps Perdue

＊

HAVING A SWILL TIME
Swined and dined

＊

BURN THE CANDLE AT BOTH ENDS
Sin til late

DEATH ROW
Hangst

*

THE CONVENT
Yangst

*

L. A.
Gangst

*

TRANSYLVANIA
Fangst

ONE MAN, ONE VOTE
Dumb oxcracy

*

THE GOVERNMENT OF
NEVER - NEVER LAND
All go larky

*

AGRIBUSINESS
To firm the land

*

GREED
Egonomics

DOLLY
Opportunity knockered

*

FULL - FIGURED
Prowed to be a woman

*

BOSOM COMPANIONS
Significant udders

*

DECOLLETAGE
Damsel in titsdress

IMPOTENCE

The eunuch of time

*

CASTRATION

The pen is not mightier than the sword

*

VIAGRA

eRxtion

*

WOULD - BE IMPLANTEE

Just re - member this

FRIGIDITY

Zerogenous zones

*

FRIGIDITY

What part of "on" don't you understand?

*

FRIG ITY

You just don't get id

*

FRIGIDITY

To go with the floe

MILADY'S MEMOIRS
One's thighs fit all

*

ALIMONY
Settling up for settling down

*

MERRY WIDOWHOOD
Ex hilaration

*

SECOND TIME AROUND
An optiMrs.

ORIGINAL HICKEY
Trilobite

✴

MY OH MY WHAT A WONDERFUL DAY!
Un - zippity doo - dah

✴

BONDAGE
He   loves me, he loves me knotted

✴

I'LL NEVER SAY NEVER AGAIN AGAIN
Prude awakening

PHONE SEX
Billing for coos

*

DOUBLE ENTENDRE
C'est trois que j'aime

*

RECONCILIATION
"Never!" she un-snapped

*

ZEN CASTING
The way up and the way down are the same

PAPAL BULL
Popeycock

*

ORIGINAL SIN
Hiss tory in the making

*

THE ANNUNCIATION
Mary go round

*

MARY TO JOSEPH
I'm immacu late

MY GUY
Intellackual

*

MY GUY II
Everybody lays the fool, sometime

*

ON CULTURAL ILLITERACY
Contemplating the bust of Homer

*

THE DOORS OF PERCEPTION
Seeing high to high

HOW TO MAKE A MERMAID
Tilt the scales in one's favor

*

POST CARD
Having a wonderful tame. Wish you were her.

*

NON - COMMITTAL EPISTLE
A luff - letter

*

HOW TO SWING IT
I'll ménage somehow

FLIRTING
Curve nerve verve swerve

*

SEDUCTION
Yearn yarn yawn

*

BONNIE LASSIE
A come - heather smile

*

THE FIRST TIME
Those thrilling days of "yes" to hear

CELIBACY
The promise of eternal salivation

*

DOMINUS VOBISCUM
Holy ciao

*

SHARD OF THE TRUE CROSS
A gyp off the old crock

*

HYPOCRISY
As easy as pious

MAY - DECEMBER ROMANCE
Mildewey - eyed

*

MAY - DECEMBER ROMANCE II
Fur - fetched

*

TB OR NOT TB
Inconspicuous consumption

*

CAMILLE
Men are only after wan thing

LIFE'S LANDSCAPE
Piques and follies

*

SCATOLOGY
Shit - chat

*

THE BIG LIE
Jumbo - mumbo

*

TANTRUM
Pique - a - boo - hoo

THUMBELINA'S PHILOSOPHY
Life is short

∗

CURSORY RHYME
Humped he Dumped she

∗

AND GOD CREATED DISNEYLAND
Put your Minnie where your mouse is

∗

EENIE, MINNIE, MINY, MO'
Polygamouse

THE REAL WORLD
Doo - do unto others

*

MODERN TIMES
Shivalry is not dead

*

SKIM
The milk of human kindness

*

FEET OF CLAY
Herosion

TOILET TRAINING I
To have shants in your pants

*

TOILET TRAINING II
Apropo - po

*

TOILET TRAINING III
To do one's doody

*

TOILET TRAINING IV
Success with flushed

NYMPHET
Belle of the bald

*

JAIL BAIT
Coke - ette

*

CHILD BRIDE
You really gottah old on me

*

DROIT DE SEIGNEUR
Sir imposition

LEG MAN
Rockette scientist

*

FARMER'S DAUGHTER'S COME - ON
She woinked at me

*

DAUGHTER' S FARMER
Plowing the back 40 - 26 - 36

*

FARMER'S DAUGHTER'S FAREWELL
John Deere letter

THEREFORE I WILL RESPECT YOU
AFTERWARDS
Phallacious argument

*

THE WAY TO A MAN'S HEART
Is through his 4th and 5th ribs

*

SAILOR'S MAXIM
There's a port in every girl

*

YES, BUT
All men should be well, hung

GEE, MR. WIZARD
You reek, agh!

*

PERMISSION GRANTED, LIZZIE
Go and axe your father

*

McDONALD'S
Burgatory

*

HEBREW U.
Halls of oy veh

THE SHY VIRGIN
Shrinking inviolate

*

PEDOUGHPHILE
The Nookie Monster

*

SEDUCER
Knackturnal animal

*

BASTARD
Son of a botch

MODERN TIMES
Truffalo Bill

*

MOMA
Salon de refuse

*

COMPUTER CULTURE
The world wide ebb

*

FOOD FOR THOUGHT
Ignawrance

INFANT MORTALITY
Pushing upsy - daisies

*

SUTTEE
C'mon baby alight my pyre

*

SUICIDAL TENDENCIES
Splat personality

*

SUICIDE
A rid - life crisis

AMERICA
McDonna Duck

*

MR. OLYMPIA
Brutey pageant

*

ROBBER BARON
Aristoc rat

*

TELEVANGELISM
Amazing grease

THE WOLF WHO CRIED "WOLF!"
You and me, bay

*

KISS AND TELL
Tryst and shout

*

PLANNED PARENTHOOD
Once spermed, twice shy

*

PENELOPE
Weave well enough alone

FALSIES
Abracada bra

*

THE LOVE BOAT
Me and U -

*

THE LOVE BOAT
Romantitanic

*

WRECK OF THE LOVE BOAT
Flirtsome and jisim

JETSETERA
Gstaad infinitum

*

THE GOLDEN YEARS
Sybarattic

*

MEMOIRS
Living life in the past lane

*

NOSTALGIA
Pasturbation

INHERITANCE

Ilk - gotten gains

*

IMPURE SCIENCE

$mE = \$¢^2$

*

PHILENTROPY

Out of alms way

*

RICHES TO RAGS

The lapse of luxury

BREAKFAST OF COURTESANS
We tease

*

COWGIRL'S LAMENT
My lips are chapped

*

AT THE DRIVE - IN
Chevrolaid

DEFLATED
Went over like a laid balloon

WONDERBRA
Cup id

*

WET TEE - SHIRT CONTEST
Show 'em a thong and two

*

G - STRING
Gnattily attired

*

FALSIES
Fool - figured

ALL'S FAIR IN LOVE AND WAR
"Fire when giddy, Redley!"

*

CUSTER'S LAST STAND
So Sioux me

*

FASTER THAN A SPEEDING BULLET,
MORE POWERFUL THAN A LOCOMOTIVE
SuPRman

*

LOIS' S LONGING
A weekend ex cape

STEAL A KISS
S mootch

*

NEANDERTHRALL
He stoops to conk her

*

SECRET SANTA
Elf - infatuation

*

MACHO
Wears his hard-on his sleeve

BABE IN THE WOODS
He left me in the larch

*

S - O - B - S   S - O - B - S
Remorse code

*

HEARTBREAK HOTEL
Haunted ows

*

RESILIENCE
With glue my heart is laden

HOW TO FLIRT
Avert eyes

*

HOW TO FLIRT II
Be trying with all your mights

*

LATE - NIGHT CHAT
Coitus, interrupt us

*

I HAVE A HEADACHE
Procrastonight

CONJUGAL VISIT
Parole in the hay

*

REVELATION
God the farther

*

THE SURGEON
A life of slice

*

THE SOUND OF ONE HAND CLAPPING
I zen me, honest I do, honest I do

SOMETHING HE CAN HOLD ON TO
You've got a weigh about you

*

FAT CHANCE
Waist not, want not

*

THE FAT LADY SINGS
Return to slender, address unknown

*

DIETING
A waist is a terrible thing to mind

MY LAST DUCHESS
Mere whore, mere whore on the wall

*

THAT COSMO GIRL
Lhooker

*

ME TARZAN, YOU JANE, HIM CHEETAH
Treesome

*

ONECONDITIONAL LOVE
Serial Momogamy

KAMA SUTRA
Sans skirt

*

THE EX - HIBITIONIST
Peters out

*

PAPER TIGER
Origasmi

*

GOSSIP
Prattle - snake

SWEET TALKER
I like the cut of your glib

*

FAST TALKER
Urge gent

*

WHAT THE MAN WITH THE SLOW HAND
WANTS
Mo' lasses

*

OLD FART
Pedantique

CHILD OF DIVORCE
The shortest point between two distances

*

ARRESTED SPIRITUAL DEVELOPMENT
An Ompasse

*

GREEK ORTHODOX
Now I lay me down to sheep

*

DAISY MAE NOT
I'm not in the moo

GOLD DIGGER
Yacht to trot

*

SHIPBOARD ROMANCE
Will you respect me aftwards?

*

HOT TO TROT TUB
Aqua yes

*

SHIPBOARD ROMANCE II
Body and shoal

GIGOLO
Pubic servant

*

GIGOLO
Frankly, my dear, I don't damn a gift

*

WHAT A WOMAN REALLY WANTS
A giggleo

*

HOW TO BECOME A SKI BUNNY
Be caught with one's down pants

TO LOVE, HONOR AND OBEY
Vive la déférence

*

HITCHED
Slip - knot

*

LOUIS XVI
Le Roi so lame

*

DIRTY OLD WISE MEN
Oglegarchy

THE NATIONAL PASTIME

Butter up!
Curve.
Slider.

FIRST BASE
One on.

SECOND BASE
Two out. Double play.
Short stop.

THIRD BASE
Ground er. Pop fly.

HOME
Catch er.
Ump.

*

CHEAP DATE
Frito lay

*

MISS BITCH
Merdemoiselle

*

THE END OF THE BEGINNING
Love at first slight

*

THE BEGINNING OF THE END
A mouldering glance

BOURGEOIS
The love of Monet is the root of all evil

＊

SHOP TILL YOU DROP
Squanderlust

＊

THE MOST ELEGANT WORD FOR AN AWFUL
THING IN THE ENGLISH LANGUAGE
Cuspidor

＊

THE SECOND MOST
Spittoon

PREMATURE EJACULATION
The glans is quicker than the sigh

INCEST
Dad nauseam

WYATT TWERP
The okey - dokey corral

GEEK LOVE
Knit twits

VIETNAM
The Ke Sahns went rolling along

*

THE THIRD WORLD
The silt of the earth

*

SOLDIER OF FORTUNE
Cross my napalm with silver

*

HOW TO IMPROVE UNCLE SAM'S WARDROBE
a) tear - away Jersey

ON CHOOSING A SPECIALTY
Physician, well - heel thyself

*

THE CHRISTMAS SPIRIT
Ho - kum, ho - kum E - man - u - el

*

SOPRANO - NO
The trill is gone

*

TEST PILOT
Apogee whiz

TWO SNOBS
Like as snot

*

THE BITCH
Tits n' asty

*

BLAND DATE
A piece of alas

*

IF YOU CAN'T BE WITH THE ONE YOU LOVE,
LOVE THE ONE YOU'RE WITH
A proxy mate

SWEET NOTHINGS
Meremurs

*

WARBLES
Tweet nothings

*

FLATTERY
A can of warms

*

TACT
Blabstinence

VEGETABLES
A child's garden of averses

*

VIN
Raisin d'être

*

ELVIS (THE PELVIS)
Pomp and circum stance

*

IN AND OUT OF THE GARDEN
Women who love to multch

COURTING THE HEIRESS
She's a million in one

*

PREPOSAL
Will you merry me?

*

GERIATRIC GROOM
What's mine is hearse

*

THE OLD MAN AND DECEIT
The son also rises

NAMING THE DAMN BABY
Let's call it Quits

*

THE PIRATE
Booty is truth, truth booty

*

OPHELIA'S SUICIDE NOTE
I vill nod be looked on vid dis Dane

*

QUAKER OAF
Thee's a crowd

FORBIDDEN FRUIT
The nixed best thing

*

REVISION
The meek shall inherit the dearth

*

EMPERESS OF SILENCE AND
QUEEN OF SLEEP
The night is something more comfortable
the moon slips into

*

THE UNGRATEFUL DEAD
Incrates

PERMISSIVENESS
Spankless task, thankless tsk

*

EGGSPERIENCE
Lumpty - Dumpty

*

MATURITY
Old enough to know bitter

*

GET RID OF DEADWOOD
Defooliate

DAMN YANKEES
Scum one, scum y'all

*

THE FIRE NEXT TIME
Don't fire until you see the eyes of the whites

*

BALDNESS
The thins that flesh is hair to

*

TRANSPLANTS
Re - seeding hairline

AFTER MIDNIGHT
Cinderfella

*

FROGGIE DID A - WOOING GO
Pond - scum is as pond - scum does

*

ON KISSING THE WRONG AMPHIBIAN
Frog prance

*

THE PRINCESS CROAKS
A frog in her throat

LADY CHATTERLY'S LOVER
Hoe beau

*

KKK
Let's do lynch

*

CANADIAN INTELLIGENCE AGENCY
C. I.. Eh?

*

FASCIST TENDENCIES
Looking for Mr. Right.

SWEPT OFF HER FEET
Easy crumb, easy go

*

TINKERBELLE'S CONDITION
The claps

*

STD
Love cankers all

*

ENDANGERED SPECIES
Sex stincts

AWESOME
Acned phrase

*

ADDLESSENCE
What's not duh... like?

*

SPIN DOCTOR
Press tidigitator

*

THE COLOGNE RANGER
Who was that musked man?

THE SCALES OF JUSTICE
Are reptilian

*

DAS KAPITAL
Red Inc.

*

WALL STREET
Green light district

*

FRANCE
Assig nation

SLICK WILLIE
State of Head

*

MONICA
But I didn't inhale

*

BONE N' SKULL
Dubya meant, Dubya meant, Dubya meant Dumb

*

UNIVERSAL SUFFERAGE
All the world's a stooge

DIOXIN
Ol' Man River, he doan say nothin'

*

MARLBORO MAN
You lit up my life

*

STREAM OF CONSCIOUSNESS
By the waters of babble on

*

THE FICKLE FINGER
For Whim the Bell Tolls

AESOP'S FABLES
Critterature

*

SEE YOU LATER, ALLIGATOR!
Money can't bayou love

*

LADIES OF THE NIGHT
The fare sex

*

GHOST WRITER
Prosetitute

FALLEN IDYLL
He put me on a bedestal

*

BAD VIBRATIONS
An icicle built for two

*

IMPOTENCE
Flaccidents will happen

*

TEARS ON MY PILLOW
He waived goodbye

PERFUME
A whiffy proposition

*

Nº 6
Chanel surfing

*

FOOTSIE
Toe tac tic

*

TRANSEXUAL
Been that, done there

KATHERINE THE GREAT
Don't rein in my parade

*

MME TUSSAUD'S
Paraffinalia

*

UNDER THE BOARDWALK
Troglodate

*

SAFE SEX
Obstinance

RESUME
To play did

*

GREY ABANDON
Devil Medicare

*

NARROW ESCAPE
R. I. have to P.

*

THE OLD TESTAMENT
Ya weh or the highway

SEDUCTION
Con quest

*

EVERYBODY'S GOT A HUNGRY HEART
Don't be gruel

*

LOW - RENT RENDEZVOUS
The beast with two bucks

*

STUPID CUPID
Adoltery

HYPNOTIZING THE YUPPIE
Just Rolex...

*

ARMED SNOBBERY
This is a stuck - up!

*

PASTEUR'S DREAM
To commit the perfect creme

*

THE MOOR THE MERRIER!
Desdumbona

CAFFEINE - FREE
Narcolpepsi

*

TABLOID
Sextra! Sextra! Sleaze all about it!

*

IMAGINE
Take it if! Take it all if!

*

VAMOOSE
To sit tall in skedaddle

THE SUBURBS
Lawn' order

*

FIRST AIDS
Boys will buy boys

*

BISHOP TAKES PAWN
Bare ruined choirboys

*

LATIN LOVER
I bed, ibid, etcetera

LOVE BIRDS
Polly want a quacker

*

BIRD WATCHING
Cheep thrills

*

DOMINATRIX
Contemptress

*

DOMINATRIX 2
Let me slip into something less comfortable

BOOGAY - MEN
Things that go rump in the night

*

LESBIANS
Maids for each other

*

AC - DC
Hereto - Hetero

*

SIMPER FI
Send in the Marlenes

BELLY DANCE
Shimmyulate

*

S & MMM
All' swell that ends welt

*

MEMENTO MORI
Long time no see

*

LA MORT
C'est la vide

SALUTATIONS

LOUIS XIV
Suncerely,

*

THE DEVIL
Sin sear ly,

*

HEDONIST
Sensecerely,

SEMIOLOGIST
Signcerely,

*

STOOL PIGEON
Singcerely,

*

MOMMA'S BOY
Soncerely,

*

HYPOCRITE
Sanscerely,

ALLERGIES IN CASABLANCA
Here's lookin' (Atchoo!), kid

*

About the Author

David Lord Porter is the author of several books for both adults (<u>Love Bitter and Sweet</u>, <u>The Silver Scream</u>) and children (<u>Mine!</u>, <u>Help! Let Me Out!</u>, and <u>Histoire de l'Ô</u>). He is a professor at the Rhode Island School of Design, and lives in Newton, Massachusetts.